TRUMP DICTIONARY
Adult Coloring Book

ISBN: 1-886522-23-5
ISBN-13: 978-1-886522-23-7

Your Free Gift...

Want some free adult coloring pages? Want access to more freebies and special offers from Kip aDoodles?

As a way of saying thanks for your purchase of this coloring book, I'm offering **THREE FREE** adult coloring Mandala designs which are available only to my fellow color-ers! These pages are not sold anywhere else and can only be found via subscription.

Plus you will receive THREE NEW FREE adult coloring pages every month. And you will receive instant notification whenever I release a new coloring book, along with the chance to receive designs available *only* through my website. Finally, you will receive special discounts on all of my books!

Subscribe to my Email Newsletter and Download Your First FREE Pages Now!

Get the details here:

http://www.kipadoodles.com/subscribe

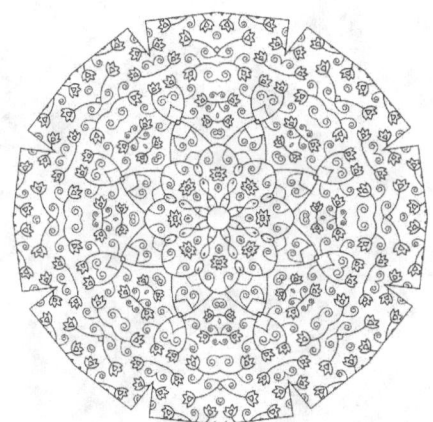 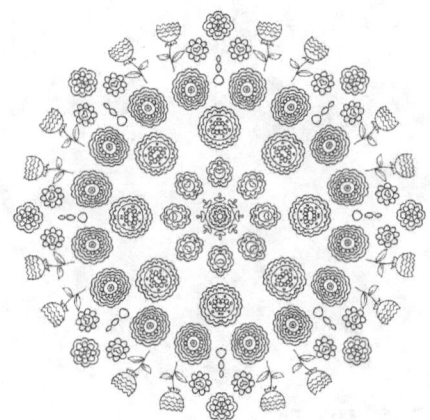 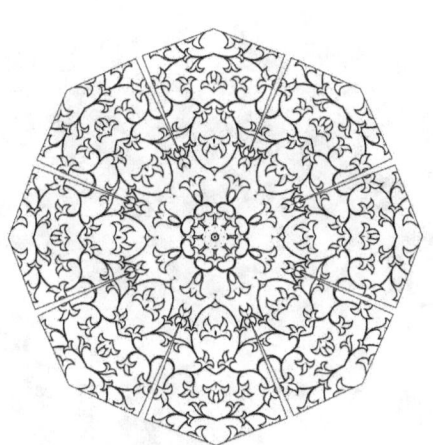

How To Enjoy This Book

Welcome to this Kip aDoodles coloring book!

    THIS IS A DICTIONARY! You will find the definitions of and quotes using the words at the back of this coloring book.

    START ANYWHERE! Begin coloring on the page that captures your attention. If it's the first design, last design, or somewhere else in the book – that's the perfect place to begin your journey!

    TAKE YOUR TIME! There is no race, no competition, no schedule. There are no "right" or "wrong" ways to color these designs. You don't even have to stay within in the lines! The only rule is that you have fun!

    Coloring is a chance to release your inner child, to go back to those innocent days of youth. Coloring is also a great stress reliever! It is relaxing, meditative, and best of all, actual restful for your brain. In fact, by engaging the right side of your brain (the creative side), it can help your cognitive health!

    You'll have hours of fun, mindful calm and relaxation while you color the 25 original mandala designs in this coloring book. Each design is just waiting for you to bring it to life with color! Escape for a few minutes or hours at a time.

    The designs in this book range in complexity, but there is nothing too intricate for even a beginning colorist to enjoy. Printed on individual pages for easy coloring offers you two benefits: The coloring will not bleed through and ruin another picture. And your finished work of art can be removed and framed, if you want to.

    Easily color these designs with any dry media, like colored pencils or crayons. You can also color with gel pens or markers. If you decide to use gel pens, markers or another form of wet media, I recommend that you put an extra piece of paper or even poster board behind the design you're working on. This will ensure the wet media will not bleed through to other designs. With the more intricate designs, you might consider using ultra-fine pens or markers to easily color the smaller design areas.

Share the experience! Have you ever colored with your family or a friend? Or with a group? Discover the joy of sharing the phenomenon of coloring! Some communities even have coloring groups who regularly meet. What fun is that!

Please "Like" my Facebook page https://www.facebook.com/kipadoodles and share your completed artwork. Seeing how the designs come to life in your hands will be great fun!

IMPORTANT: *Please do not re-sell these images.* If you are interested in licensing my art or any type of commercial, educational or non-profit use, please email me at Kip@KipADoodles.com. I would love to hear from you!

Any questions or suggestions? Don't hesitate to email me Kip@KipADoodles.com.

Happy coloring!

Kip@KipADoodles.com

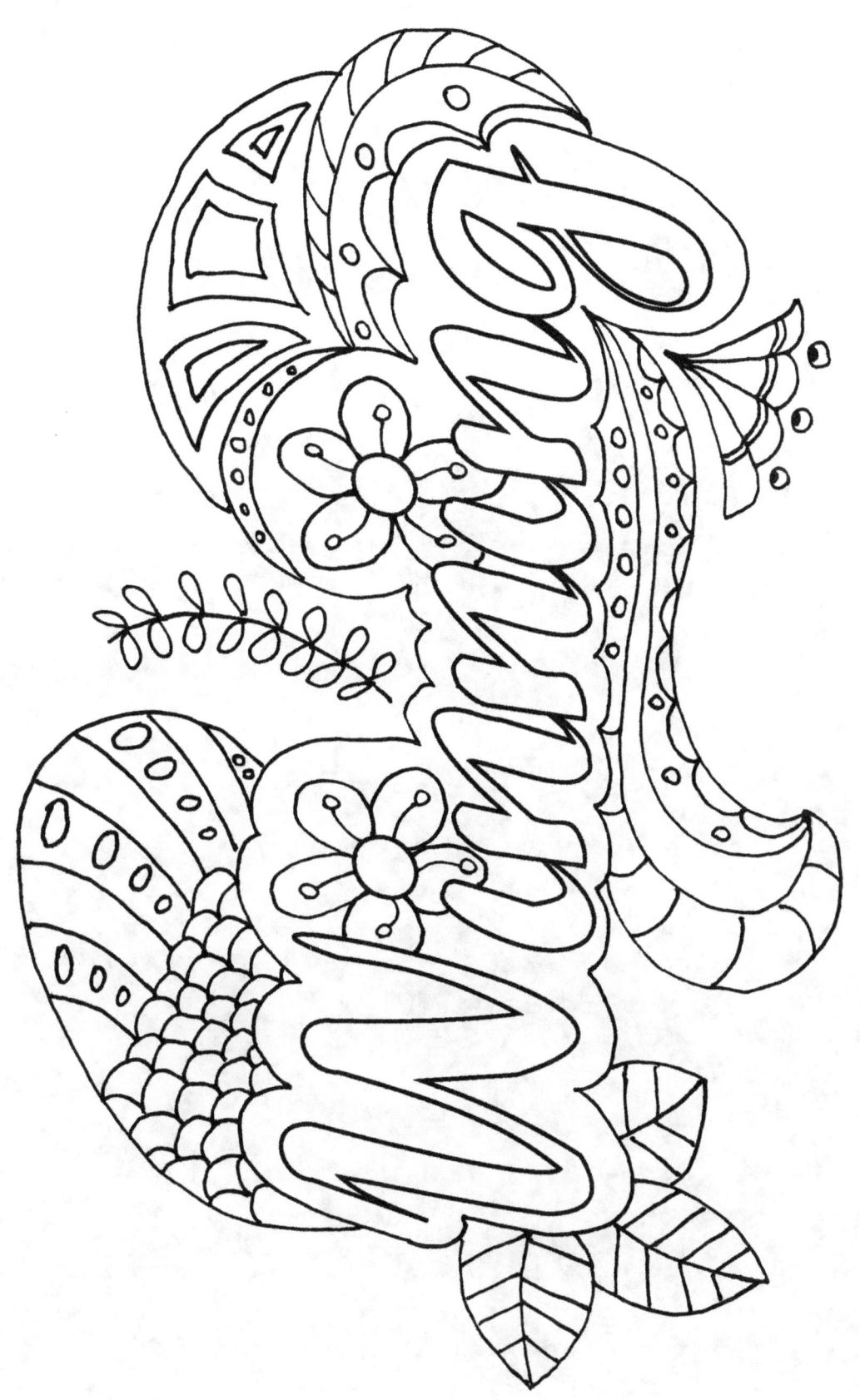

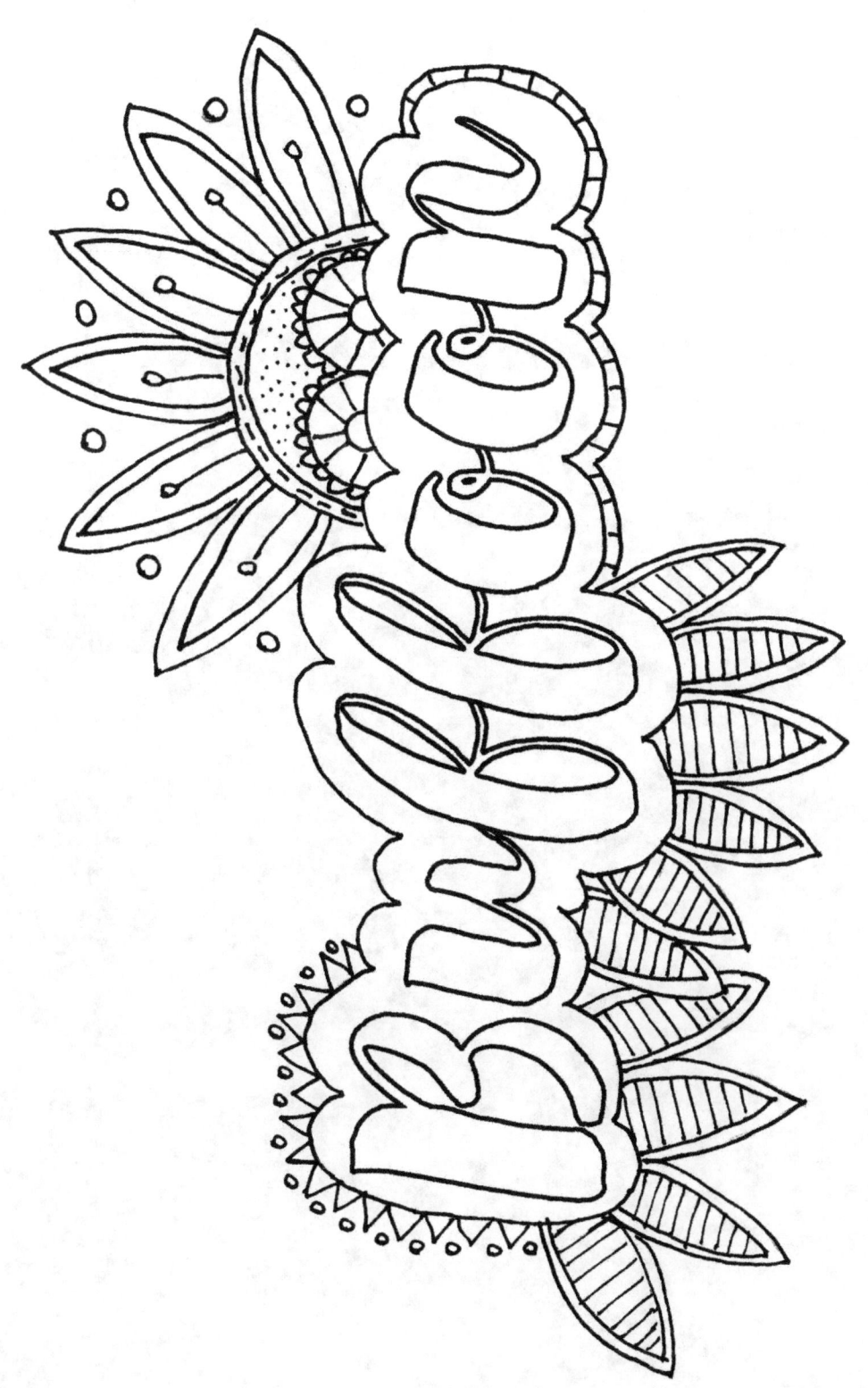

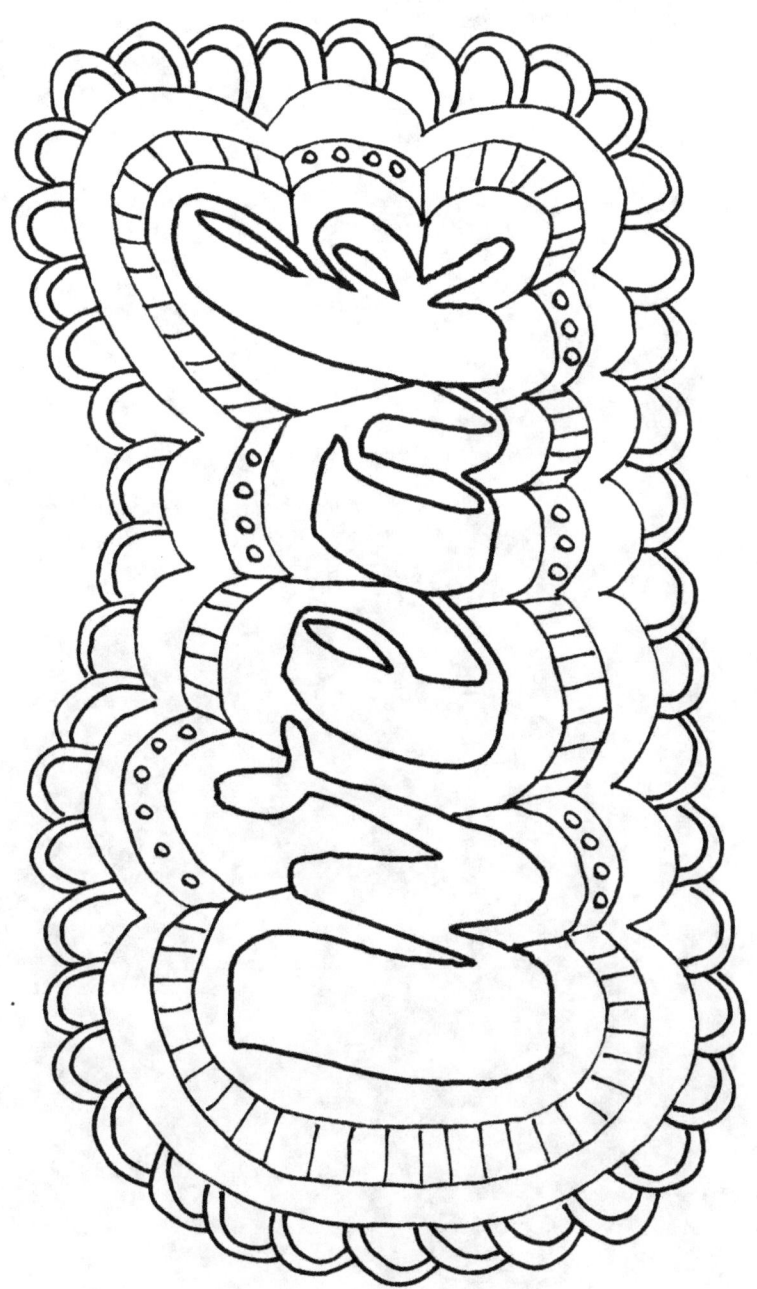

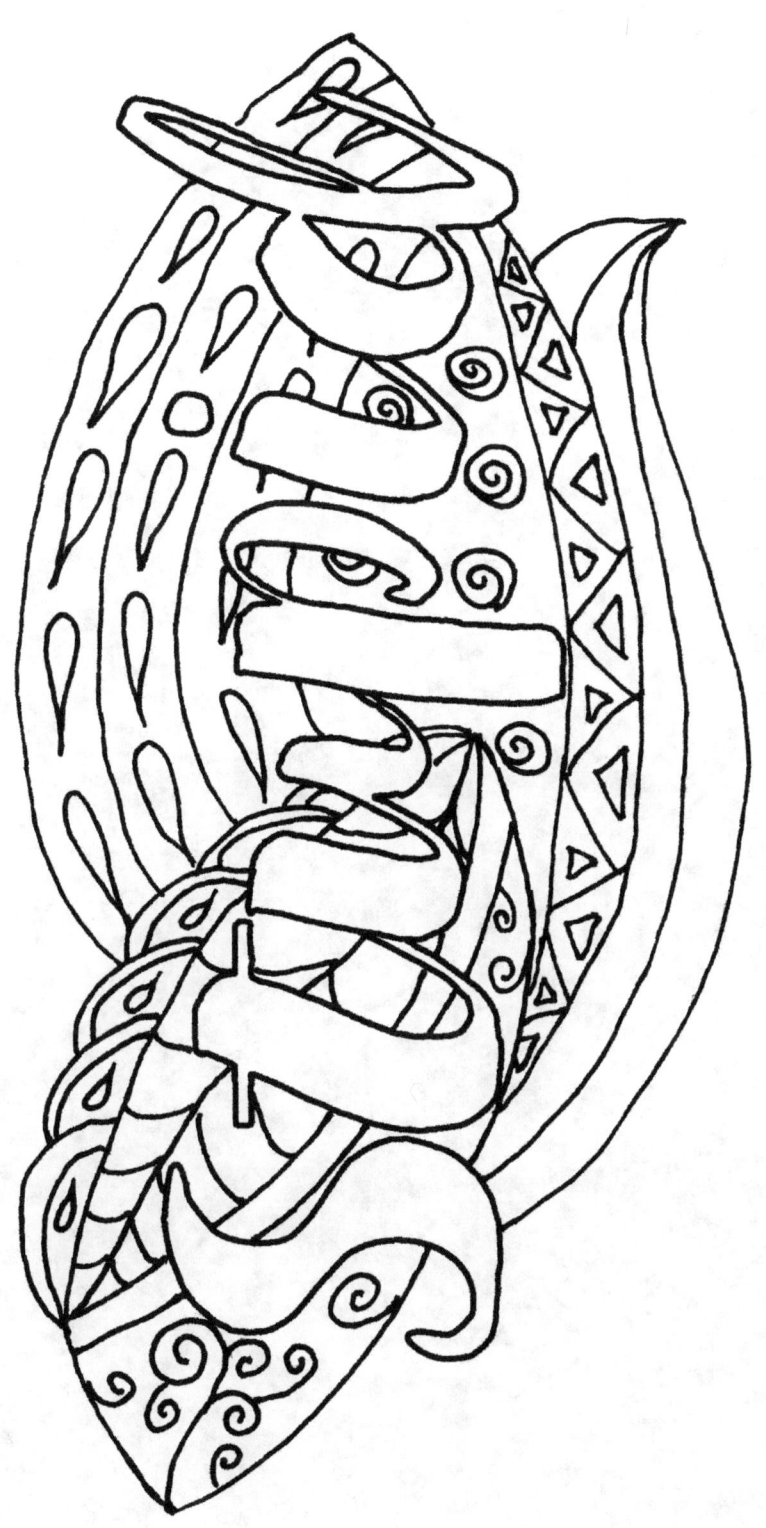

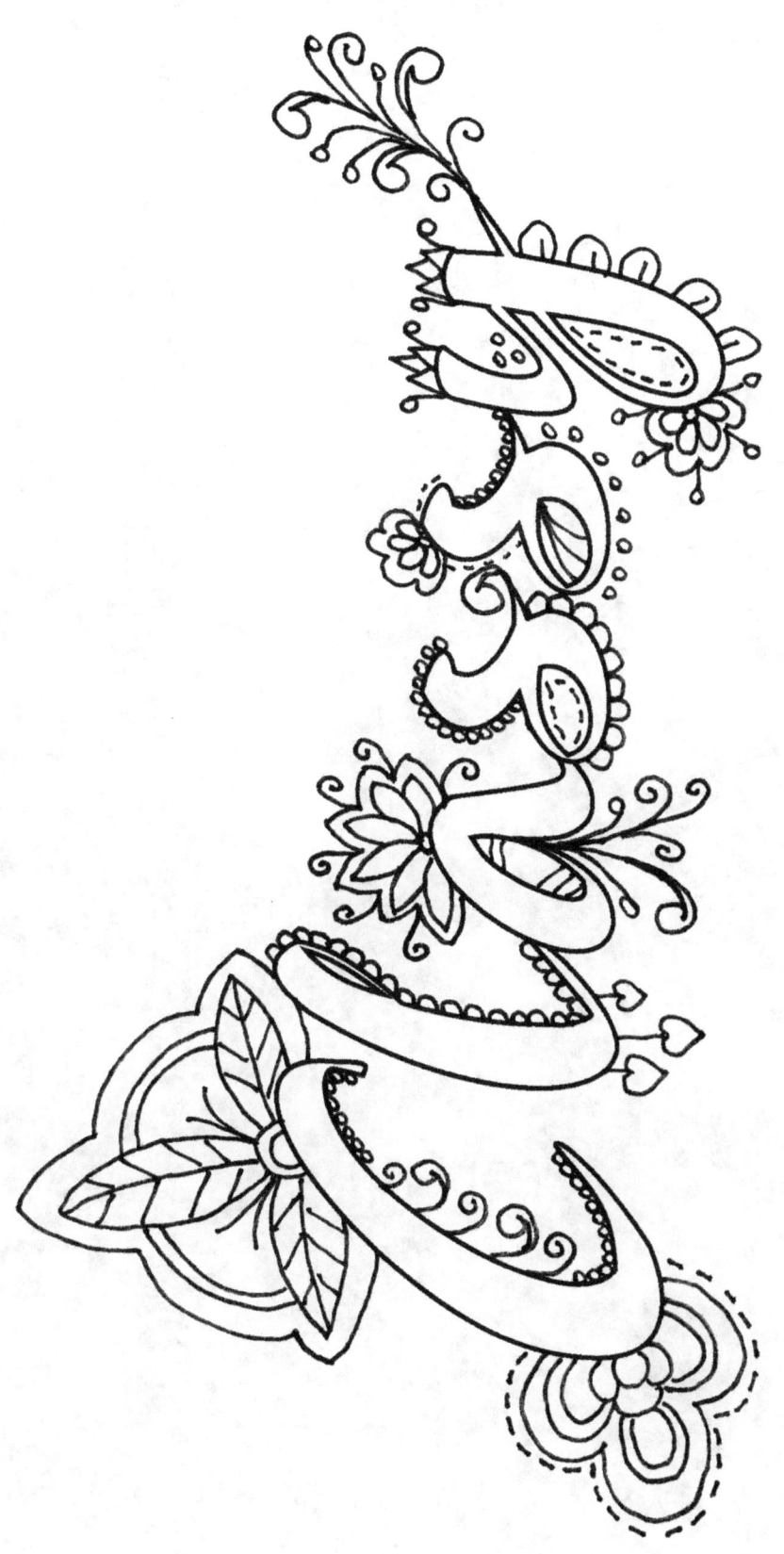

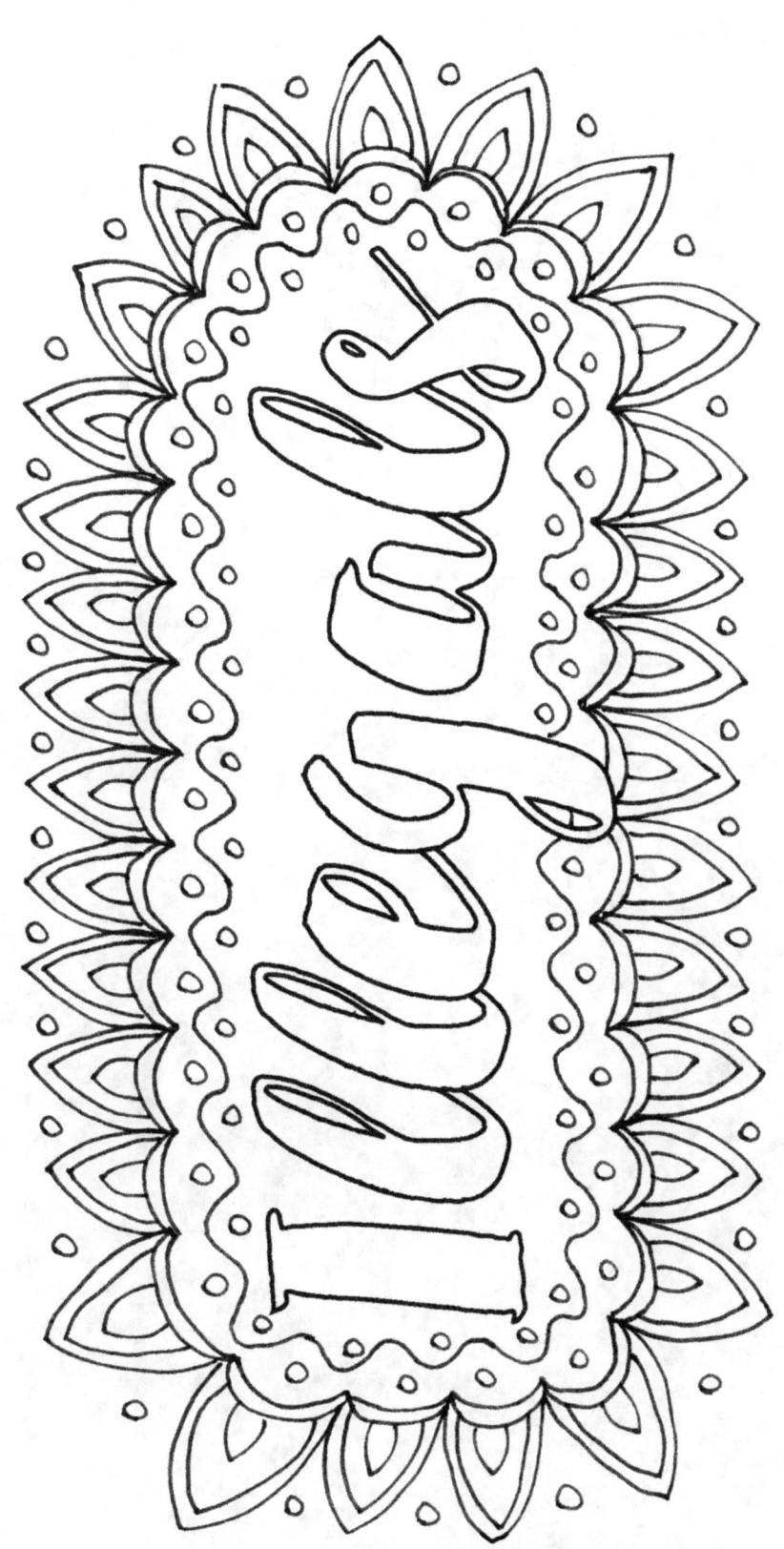

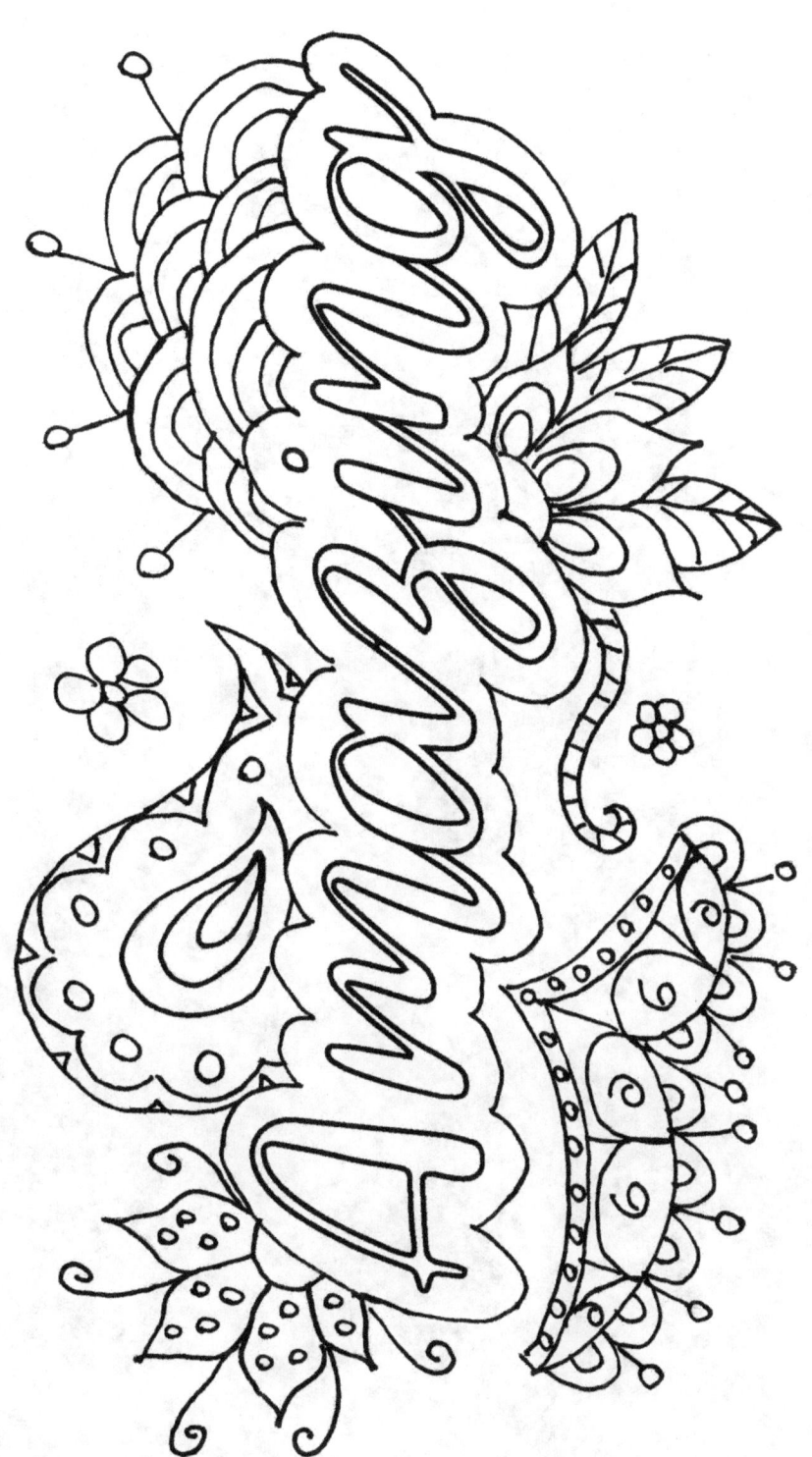

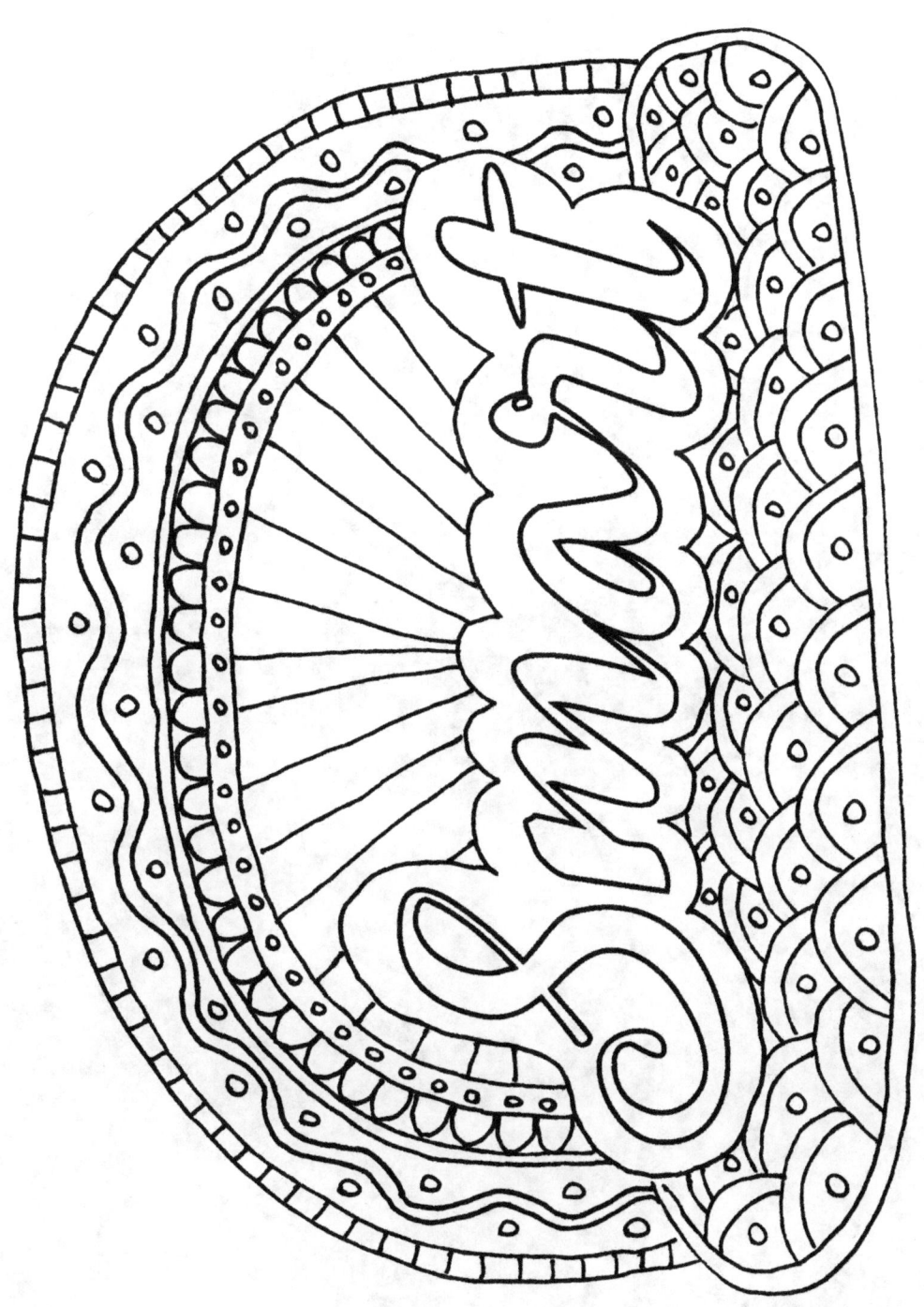

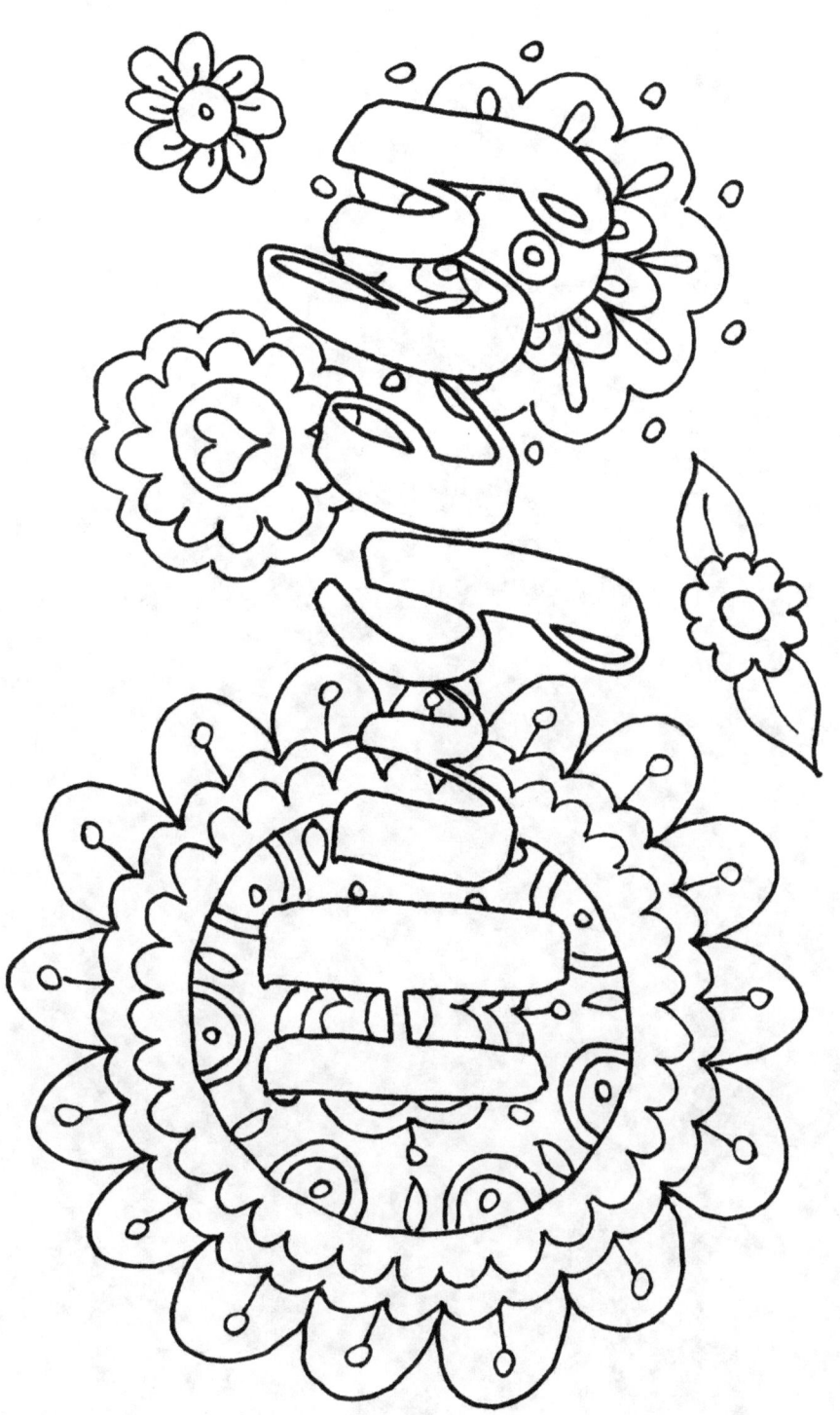

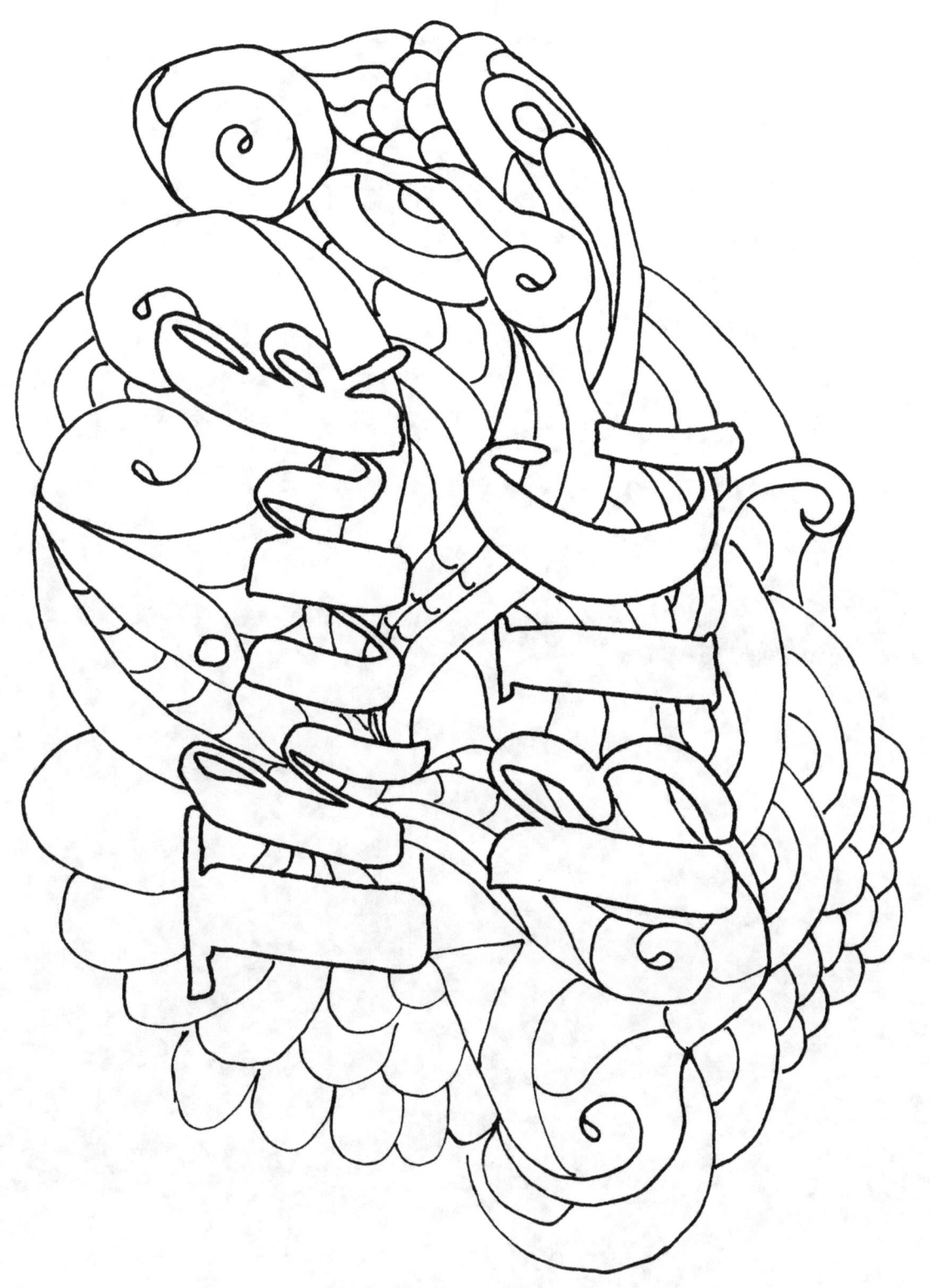

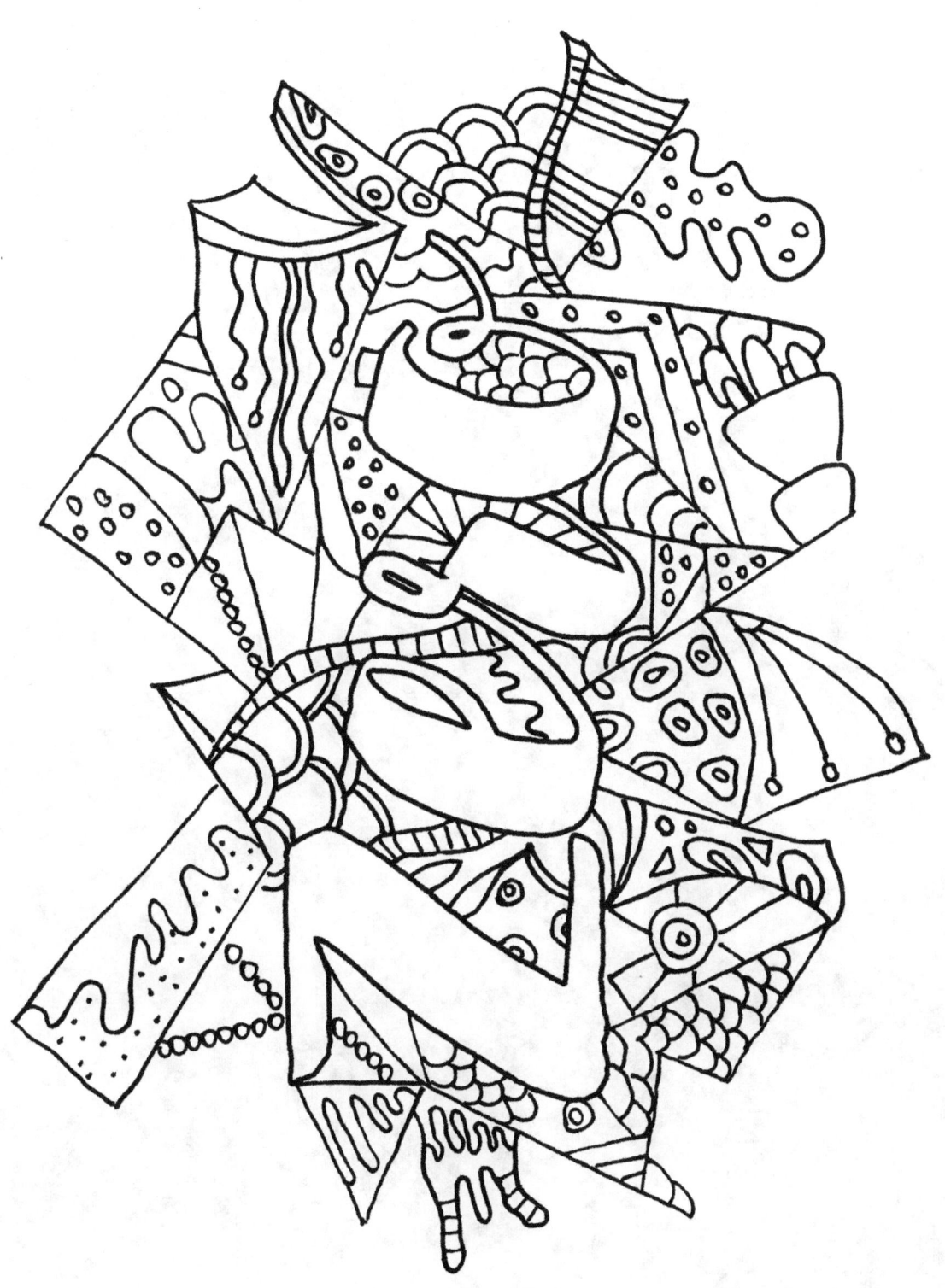

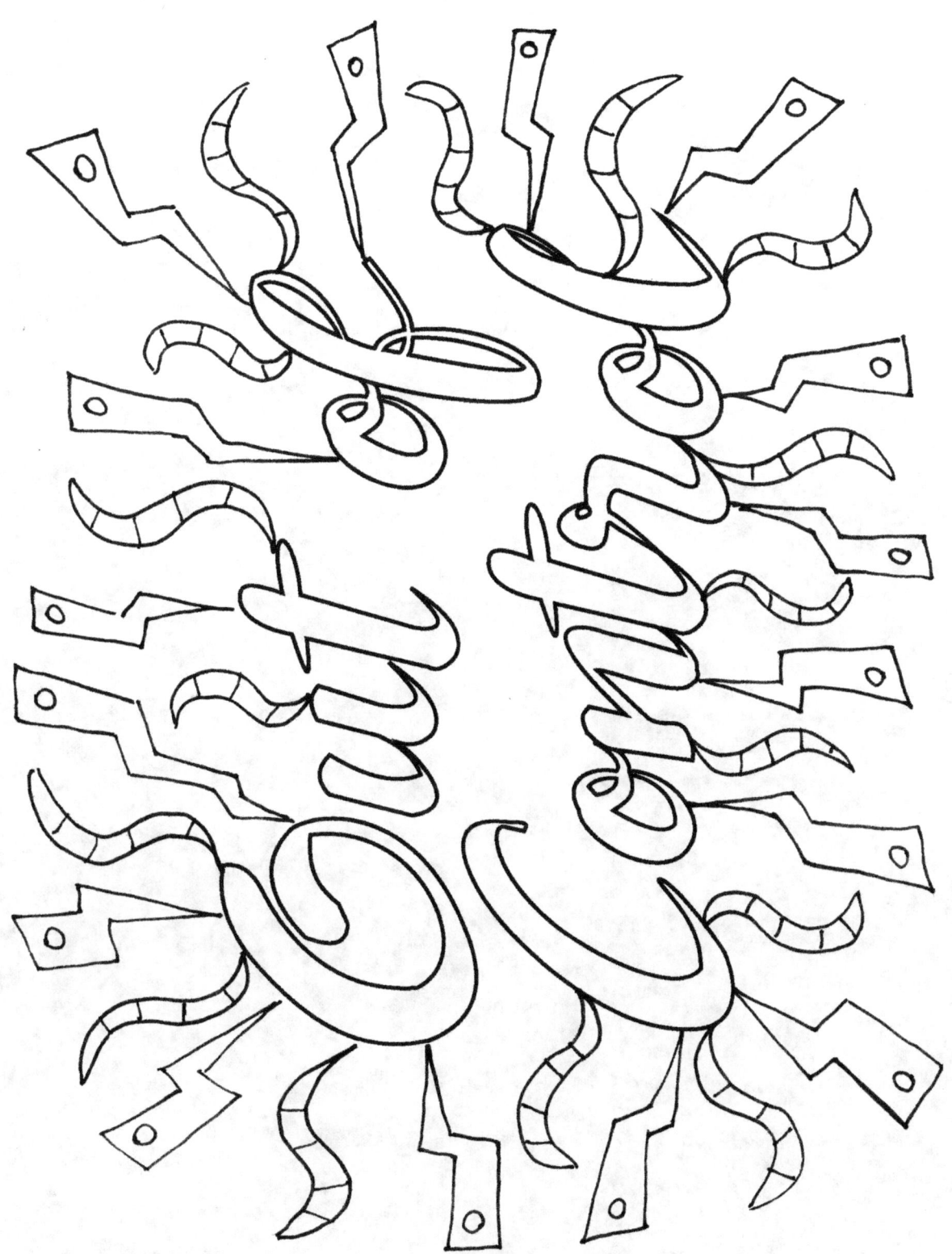

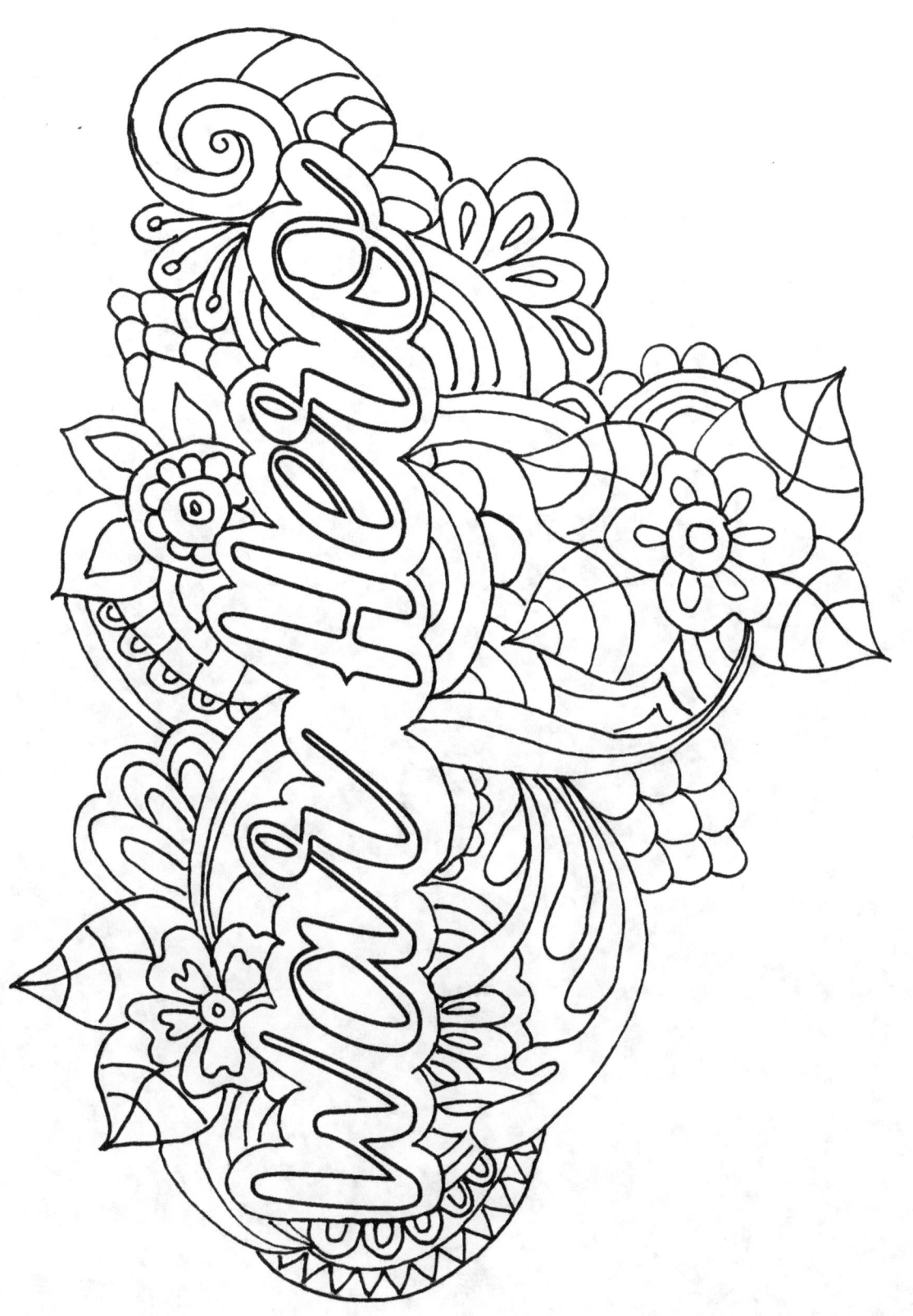

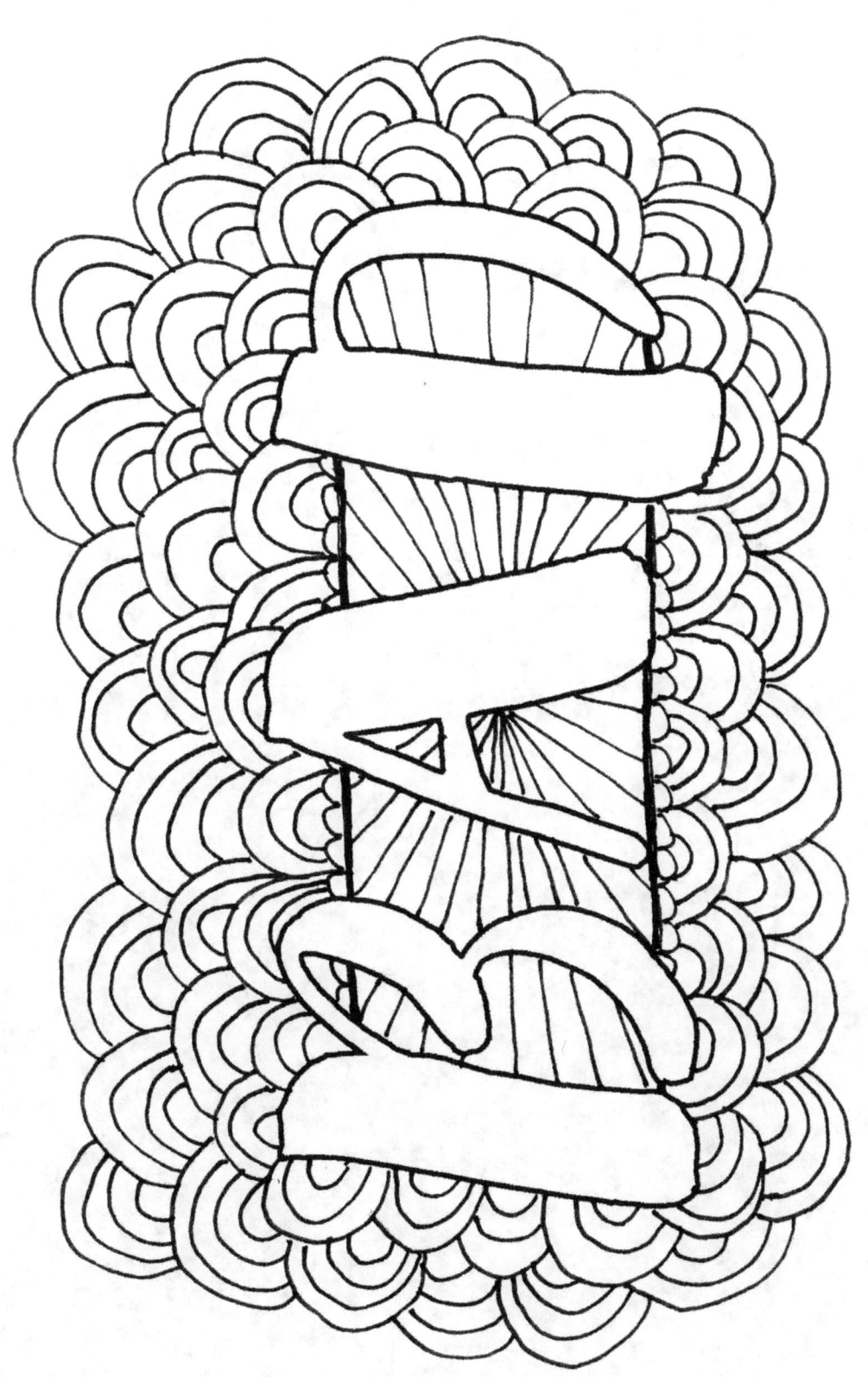

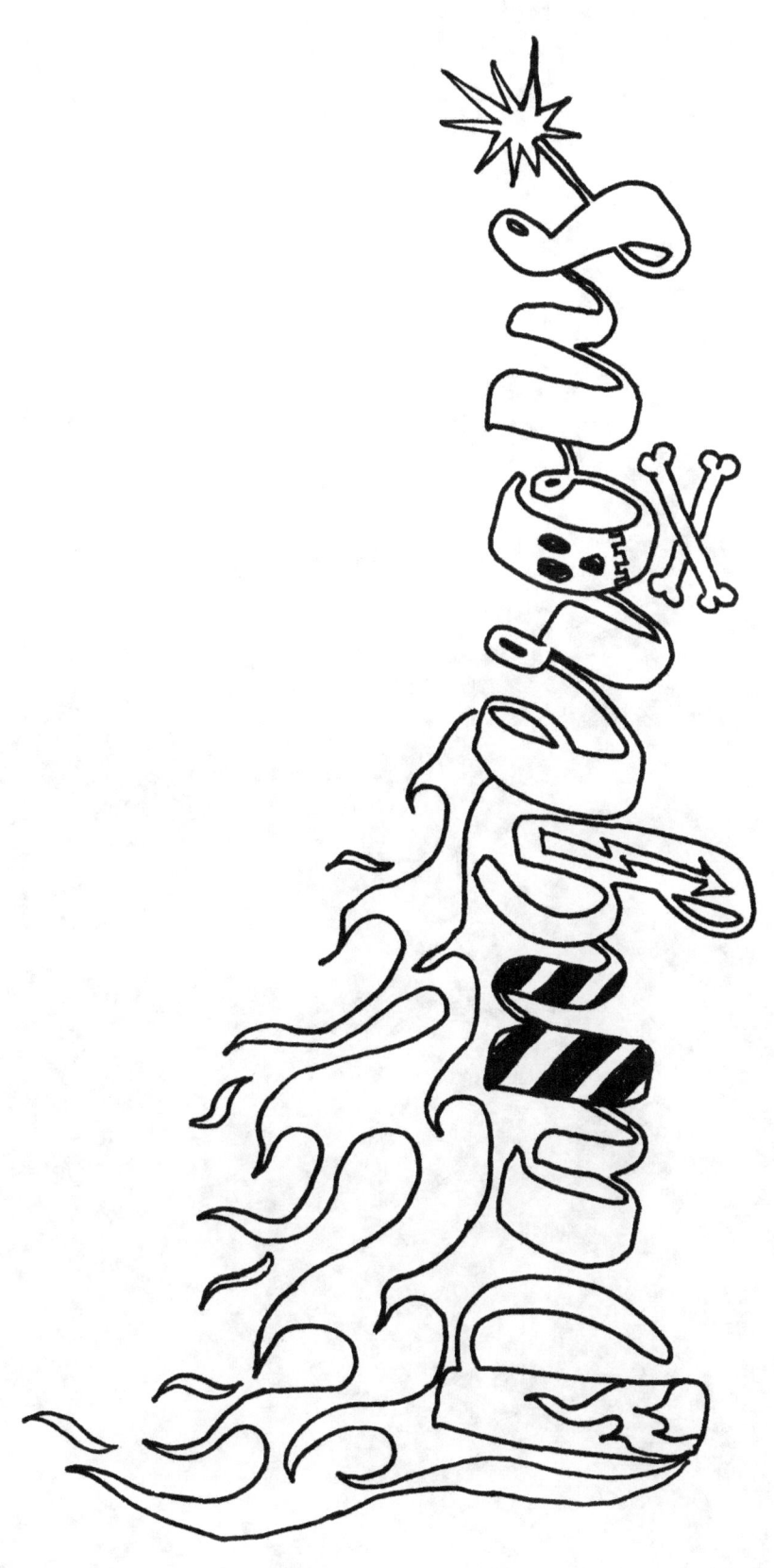

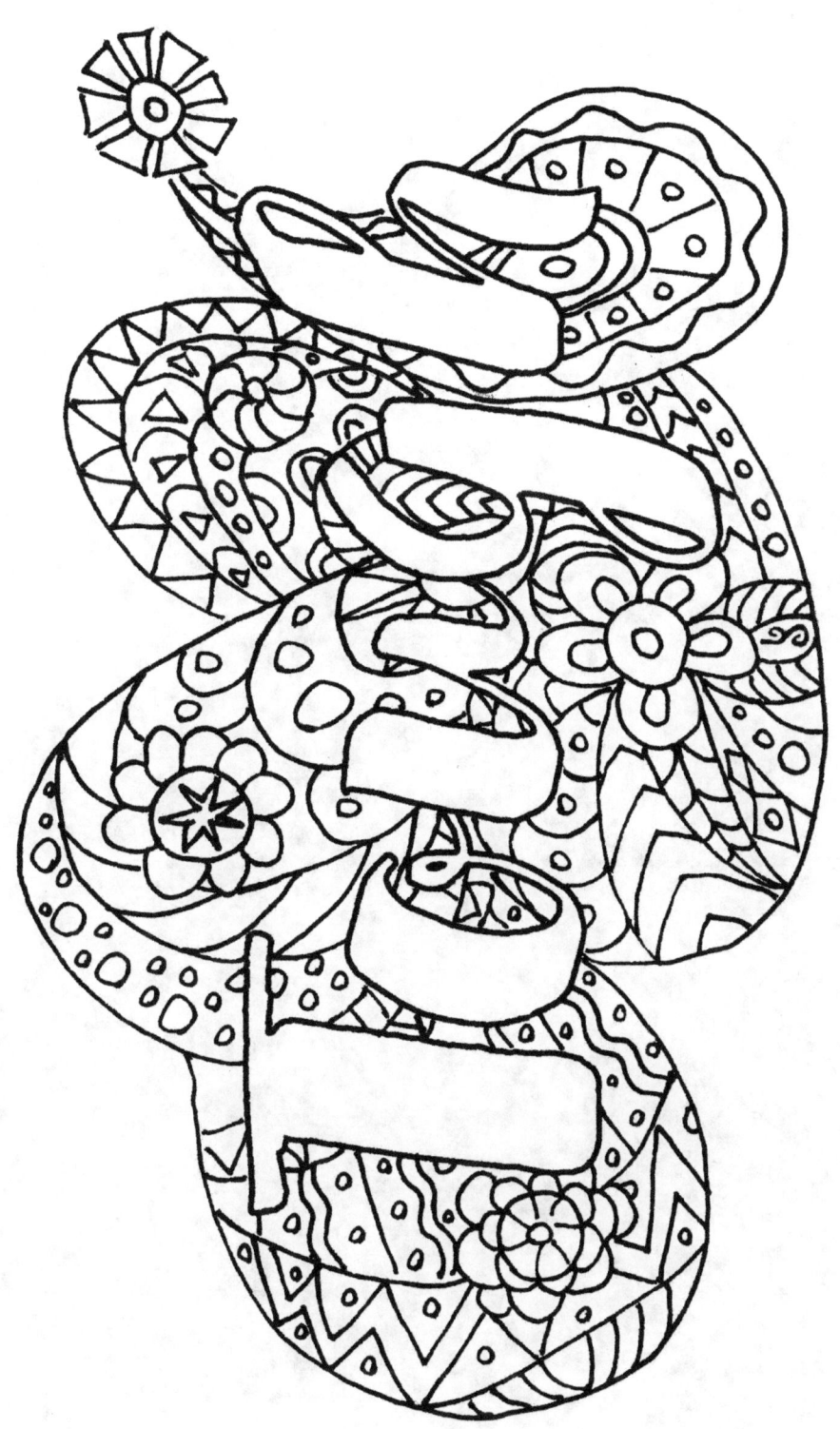

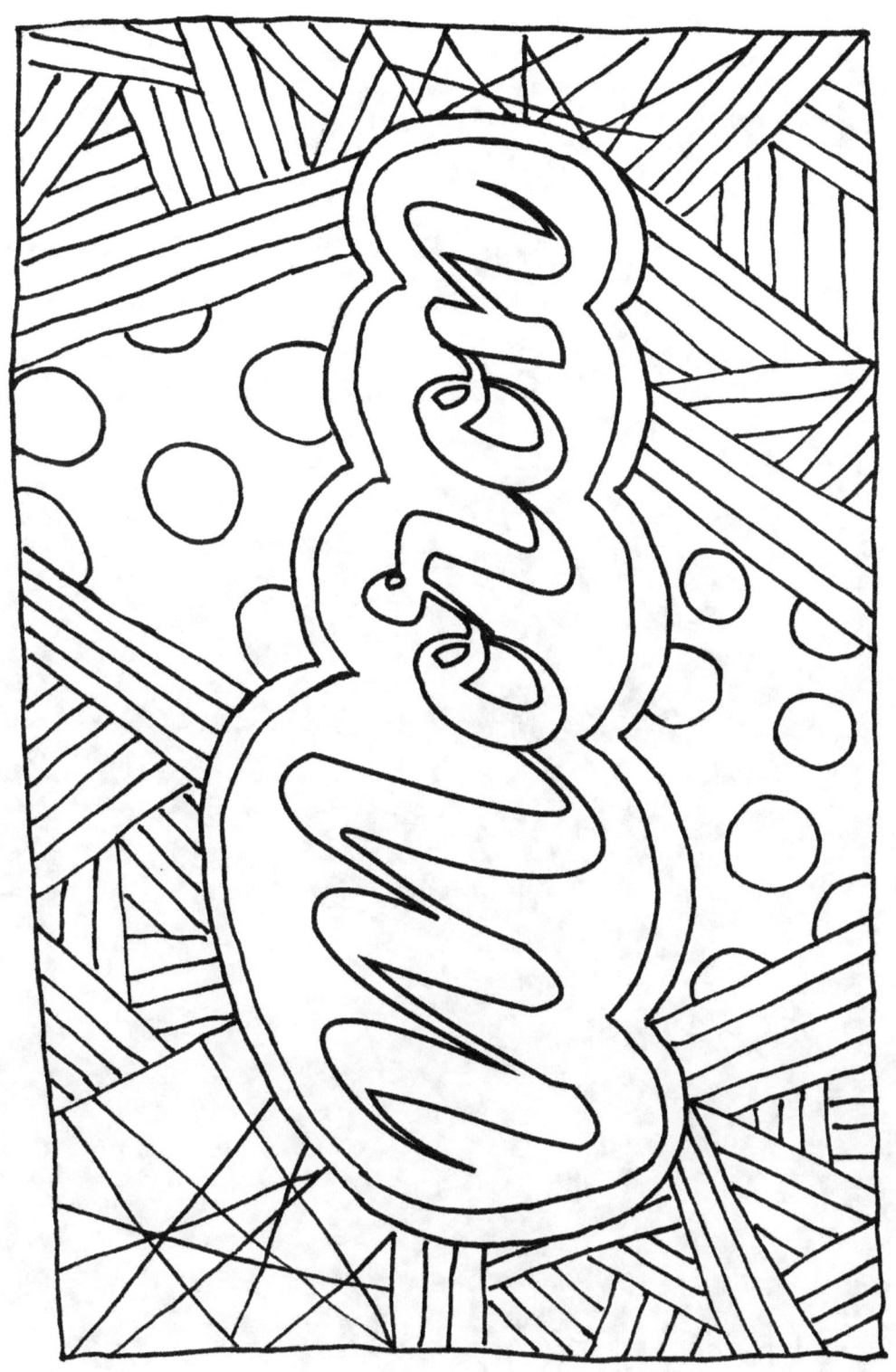

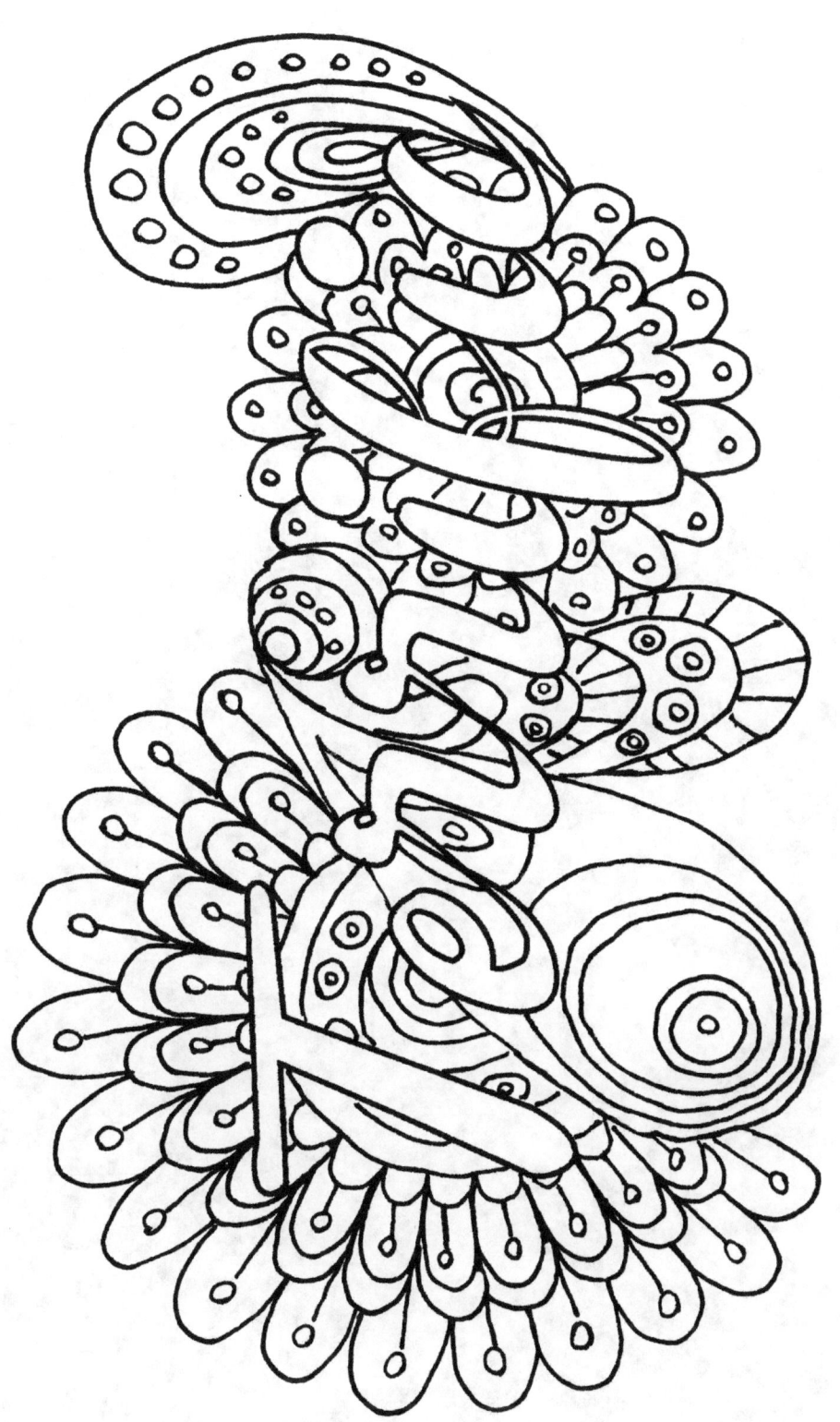

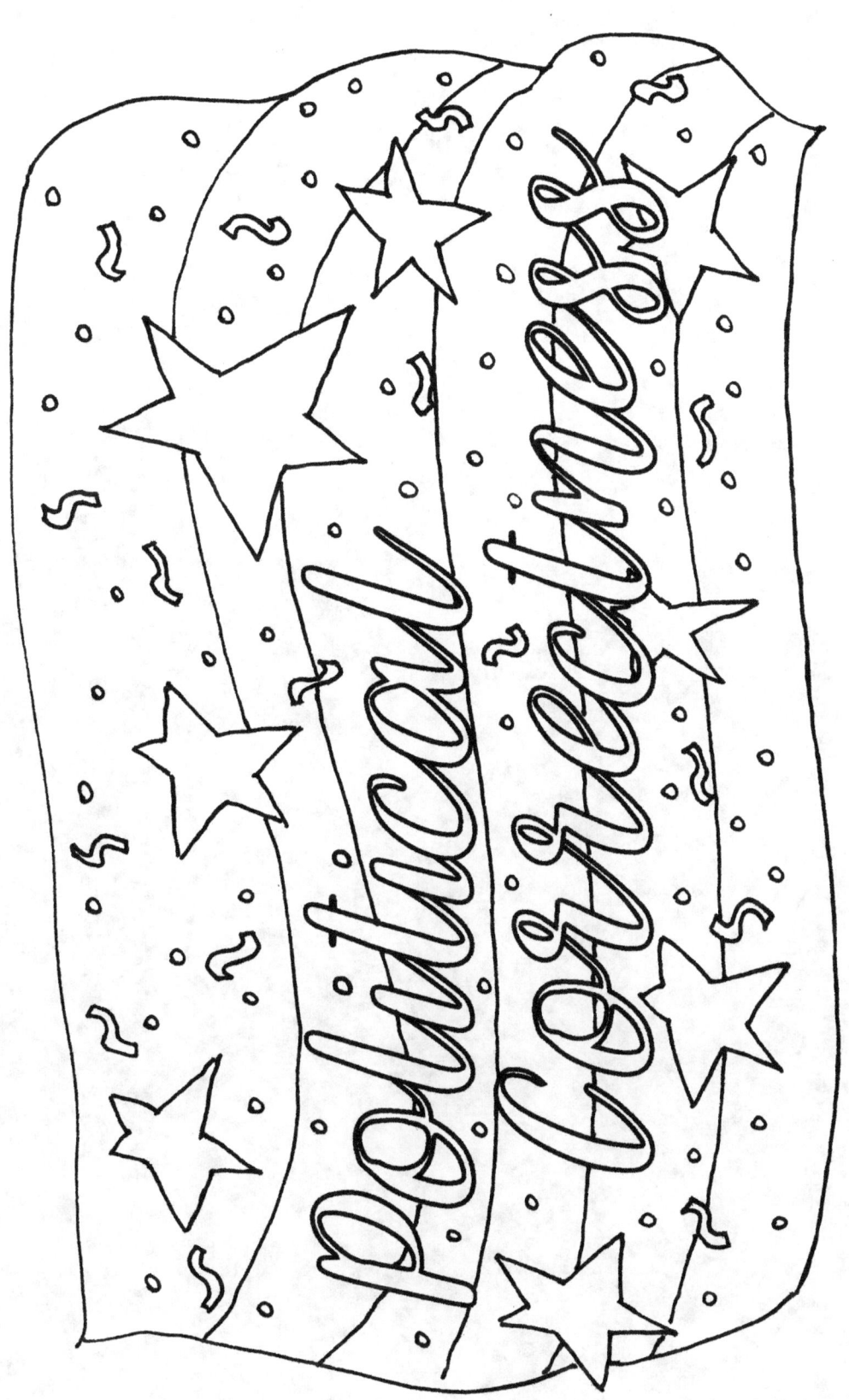

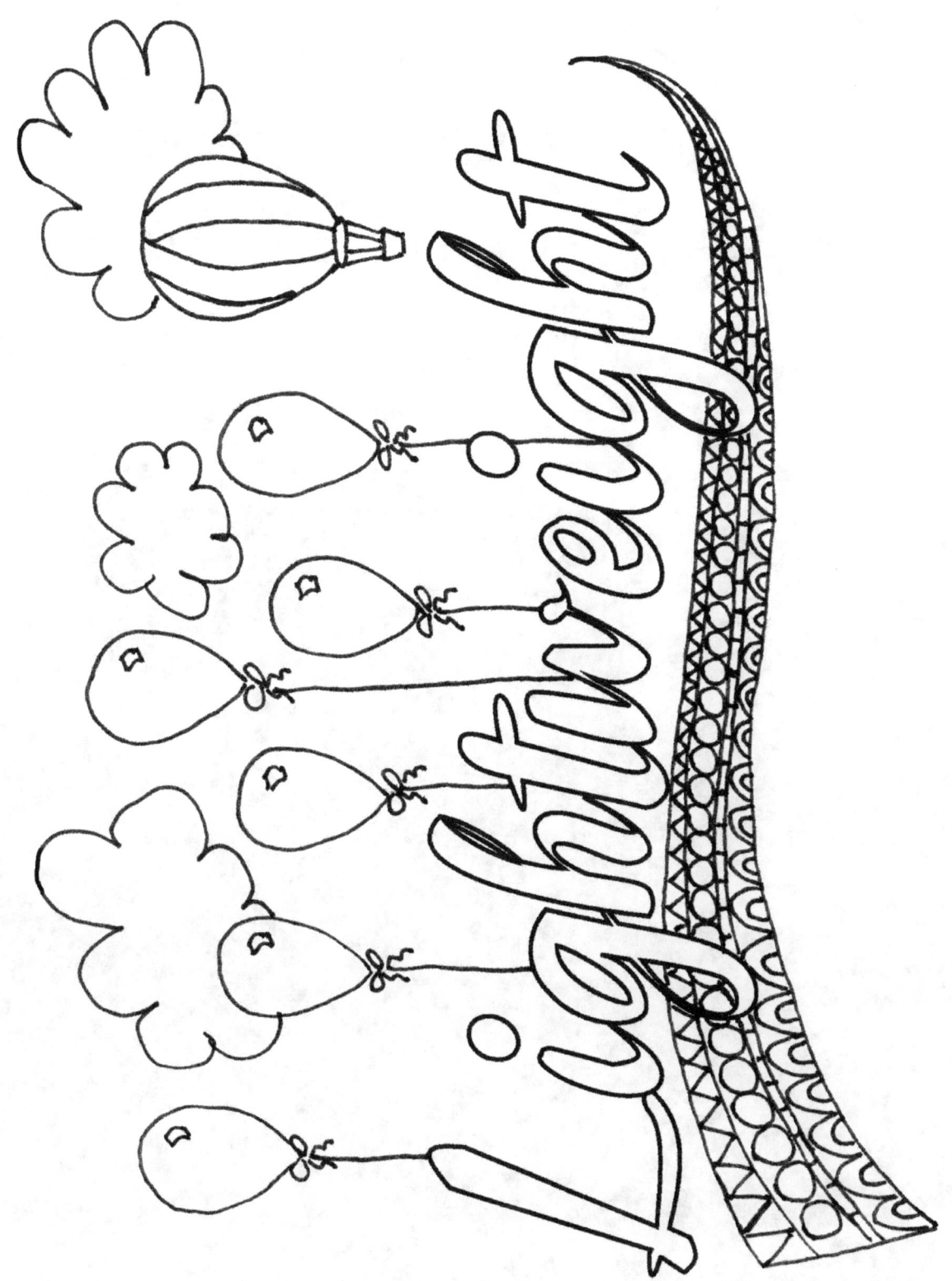

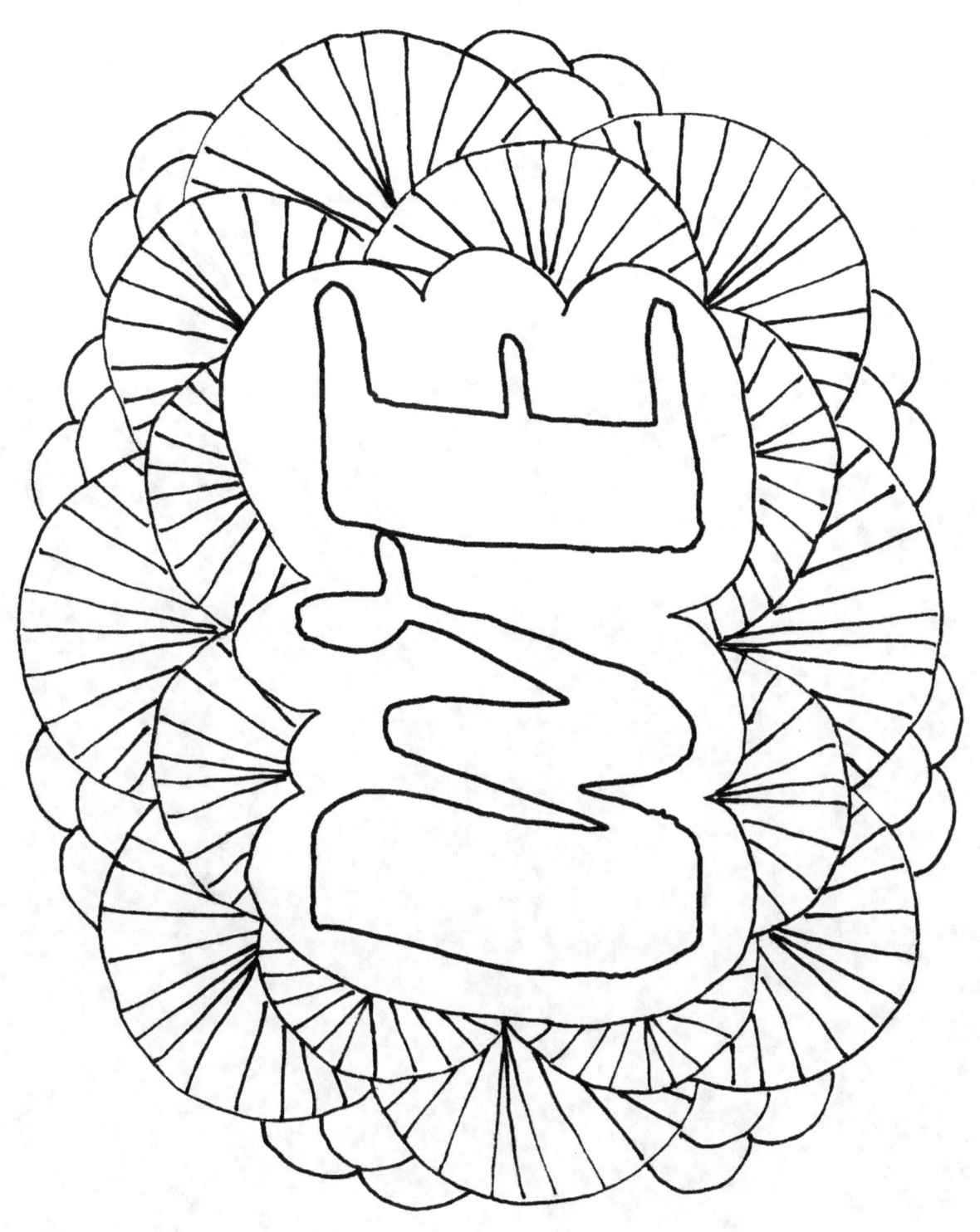

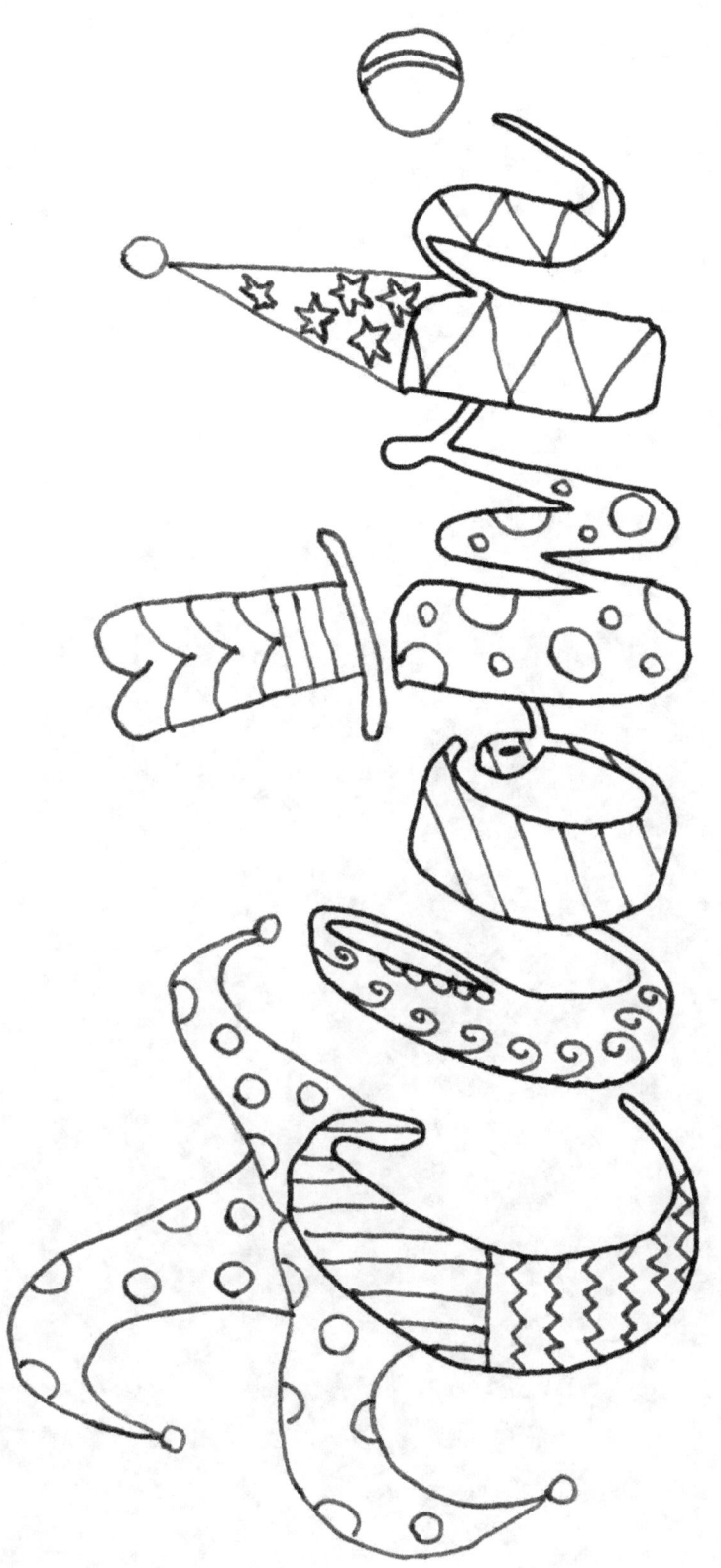

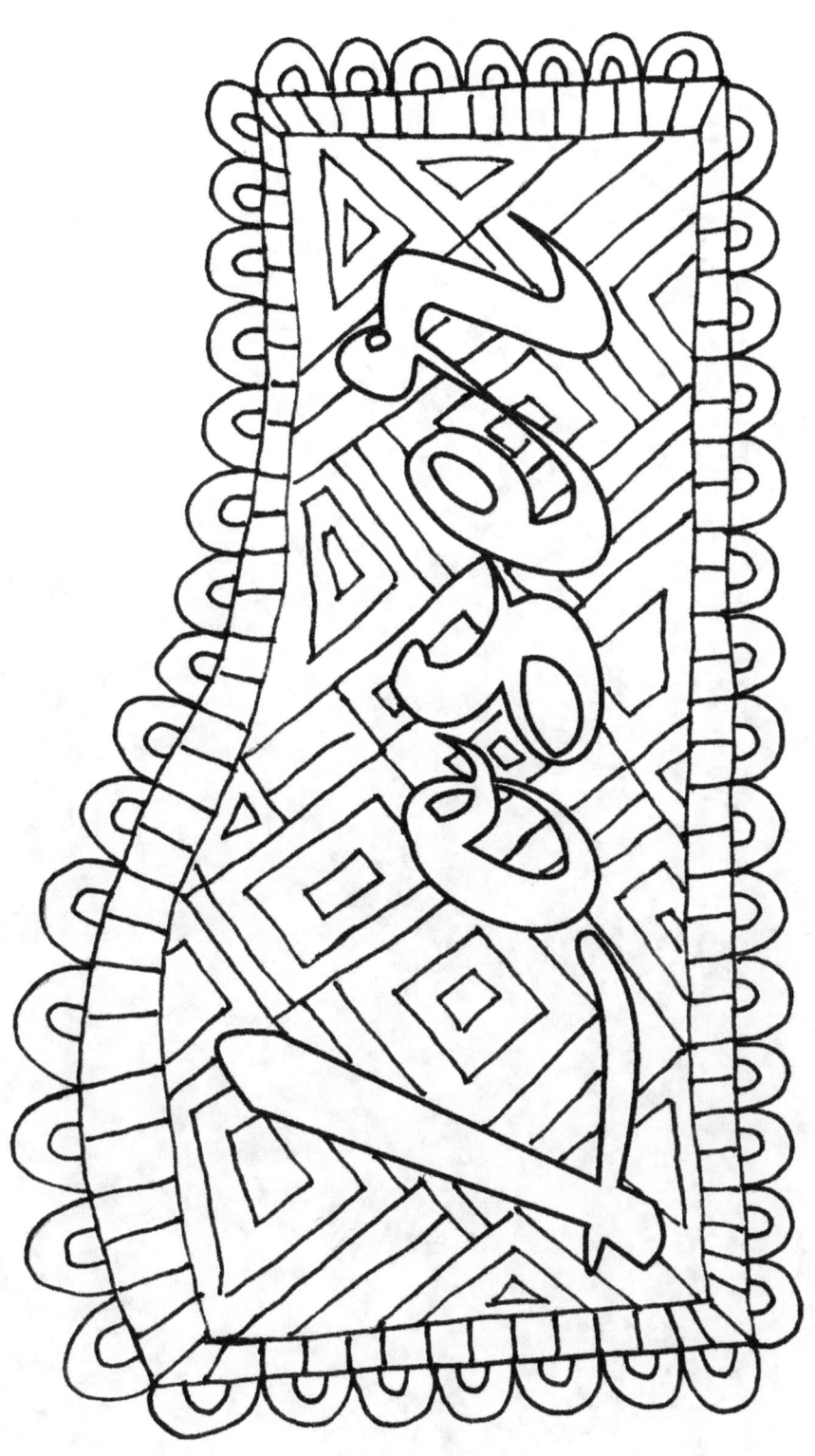

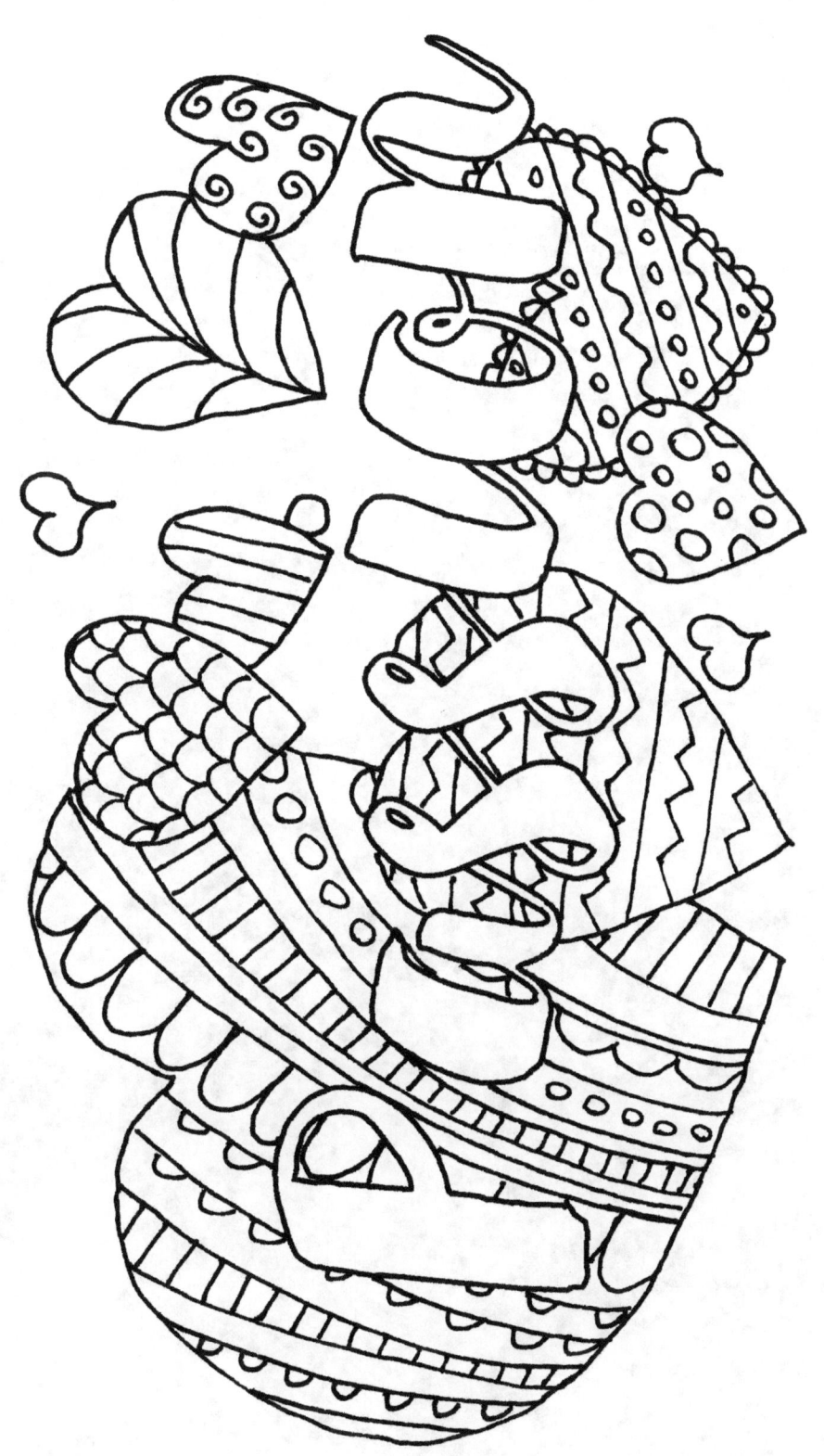

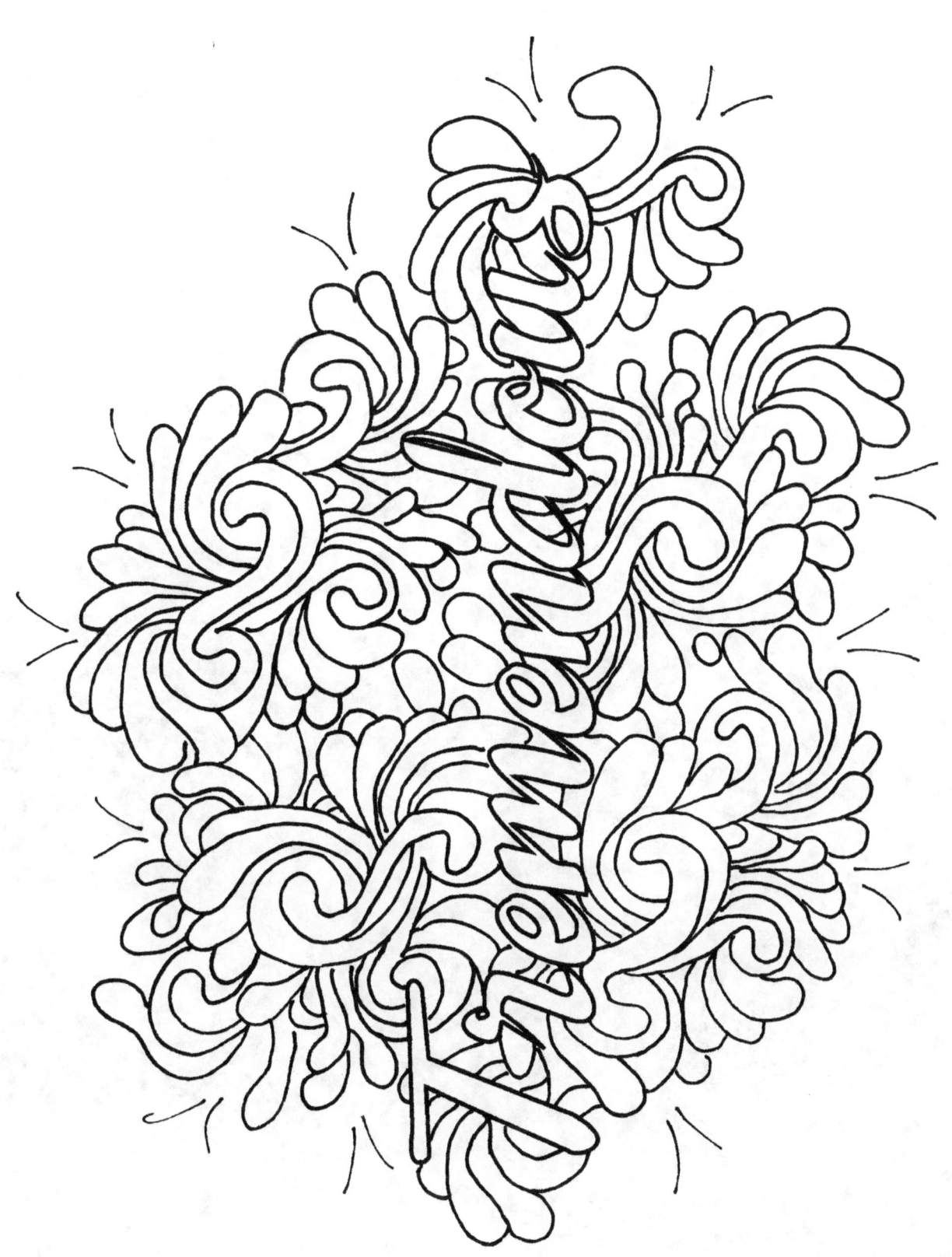

Trump Dictionary

amazing (adj.): The opposite of a loser. *See classy.* *

bad : "Something bad is happening."**

buffoon (n.): A word low-energy people allegedly use to describe winners like Donald Trump. *See clown.* *

classy (adj.): Anything topped with mahogany; any and all golf courses owned and operated by Donald Trump; anything generally excellent; the necklace you give your third wife.*

clown (n.): A word that haters and losers use to describe great guys like Donald Trump.*

dangerous : "Something really dangerous is going on."**

huge(ly) (adj.): A generally excellent thing that is impossible to ignore. *

illegals (n.): Undocumented immigrants; criminals spreading Ebola; the people you have to build a wall to keep out.*

lightweight (n.): An inconsequential person. *See loser.* *

loser (n.): Everyone who disagrees with Donald Trump; a person who is rendered useless by his inability to help increase the value of Donald Trump's brand; what Donald Trump will be if he doesn't win the 2016 presidential election.*

moron (n.) *See loser.* *

out of control : "...we're going to have to set up a new -- a new coalition, a new group of -- of the countries to handle terrorism, because terrorism is out of control."**

passion : "With out passion you don't have energy, with out energy you have nothing."***

political correctness : "Political correctness is killing our country."**

smart : "We have to be much smarter, or it's never, ever going to end."**

stupid : "I went to an Ivy League school. I'm highly educated. I know words. I have the best words, I have the best, but there is no better word than stupid. Right?"**

terrific (adj.): A word that compresses the sublime classiness of Donald Trump's ideas and friends into three syllables.*

tough (adj): "Mike Tyson endorsed me. You know, all the tough guys endorse me. I like that. OK?"**

tremendous : "I have had tremendous success."**

war hero (n.): Someone who doesn't get captured.*

we : "We will make America strong again. We will make America proud again. We will make America safe again. And we will make America great again."***

weak : "I am strong; politicians are weak."**

winning (n.): The only word that will exist under President Trump, which seems like it might be monotonous, but you definitely won't get bored.*

zero (adj.): The number of chances Carly Fiorina has to win the Republican nomination; the probability that someone who is worth less than Trump's Gucci store will become president.*

* Excerpted from *New York Magazine's* article "A Major, Super-Classy List of Donald Trump's Favorite Words and Phrases, for Everyone Who Is Not a Loser", December 15, 2015
http://nymag.com/daily/intelligencer/2015/08/donalds-dictionary.html

** From YourDictionary.com
http://www.yourdictionary.com/slideshow/donald-trump-20-most-frequently-used-words.html#ezu1VobbeIbJAFvF.99

*** From BrainyQuote.com
https://www.brainyquote.com/quotes/quotes/d/donaldtrum754622.html

Coloring Companions Resources

Visit my website for a list of suggested resources to increase your coloring enjoyment!

KipADoodles.com/resources

Have coloring accessories that you love?
Let me know about them at
Kip@KipADoodles.com and I'll add them to the Resources list on my website!

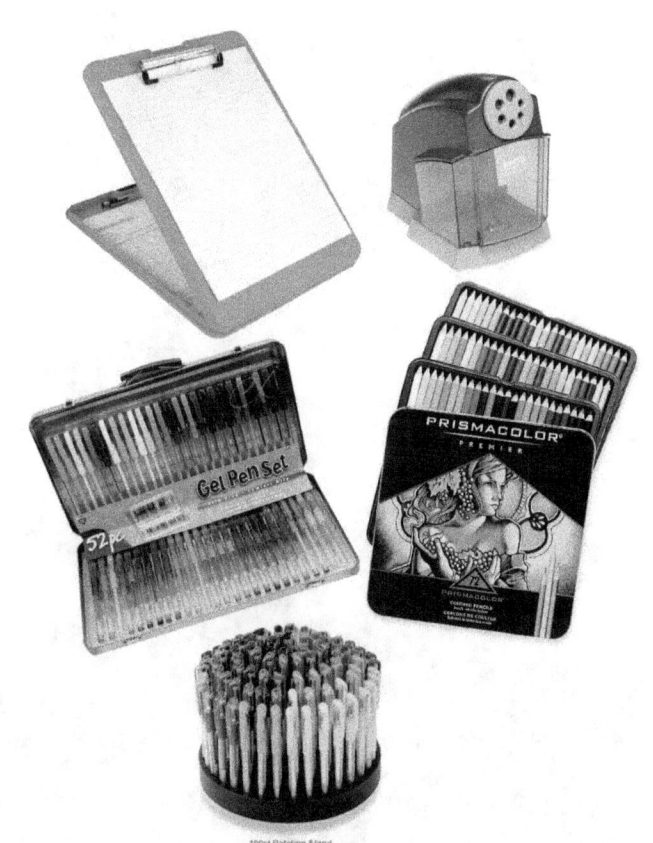

Kip aDoodles Coloring Books

REMEMBER: For Kip aDoodles News, Latest Coloring Books, and Special Discounts, **SUBSCRIBE HERE >> http://kipadoodles.com/subscribe**

Visit my Etsy store these and more of my coloring books for your coloring enjoyment!

KipADoodles.Etsy.com

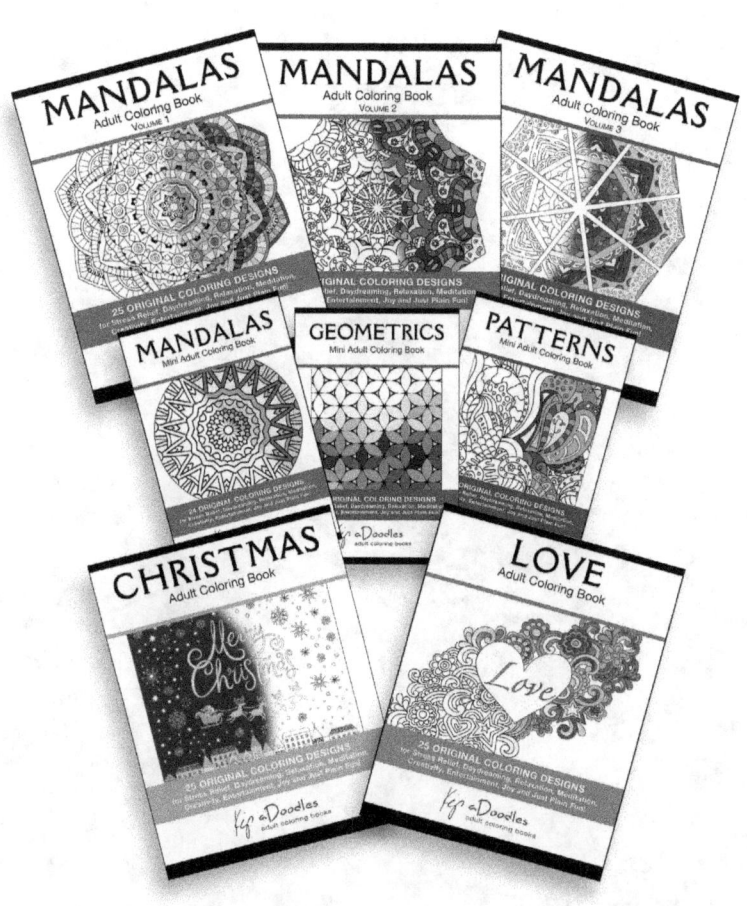

Now a Request From The Author

Did you enjoy this book?

If so, I have a small favor (that would mean a lot to me) to ask...

Would you take just a minute to leave an honest review? (Pretty please with a cherry on top!)

Just a sentence or two that tells people what you liked about this coloring book. Your words and stars will go a long way towards letting other colorists know they'll like this coloring book, too!

Did I mention pretty please with a cherry on top?

Here's the direct link:

http://www.amazon.com/product-reviews/1886522235

Happy coloring!

About The Author

Kip has been drawing, coloring and doodling since she could hold a pencil. Or more likely a crayon...Ha ha! Since then she has found many outlets for her design creativity, including as a web designer since 1993 (Yes, 1993!).

She has worked in just about every media - from embroidery to crewel to sewing to cross stitch to needlepoint to painting to drawing to jewelry design to counted cross stitch design... and more!

Bright colors, clean - and fun - designs are her passion! She also loves when the completed item is visually interesting, joyful and beautiful.

In her drawing for adult coloring books, she tries to create entertaining, intricate patterns and designs that spur the imagination and inspire the heart – as drawing inspires hers.

Kip lives on the road – and has since May 2013. She loves the fun adventure, great experiences, new friends, and endless inspiration!

www.ingramcontent.com/pod-product-compliance
Lightning Source LLC
Chambersburg PA
CBHW081628220526
45468CB00009B/2352